Something to Ponder

Books by the same author

The Meeting,
teachings of the shaman Joshua.
(A novel)

Uncommon Reason,
a novel of peace in time of conflict,
turmoil and terror.

Like a large immovable rock.
(A Festschrift in appreciation of the
Advaita Master, Ramesh S. Balsekar)

Reviews

Like the happy, peaceful murmur of a stream, the wisdom and truth found in the verses of Colin Mallard's "*Something To Ponder*," cascade effortlessly and ever so gently into our hearts, there to remain in the silence of direct understanding. Articulating the way with ease, poise, serenity and complete assurance, Colin's own profound understanding and creative quietism shine forth on every page. If you yearn for peace, this is the book to read, perhaps just a page at a time, so as to savor the blessings served verse after verse.

Madhukar B. Thompson, Author of the "*The Odyssey of Enlightenment*, rare interviews with enlightened masters." Maui, Hawaii. USA

For me the most insightful suggestions for living have come from "*The Way of Life*," by Lao Tzu. This new volume, based on the passages of the original book, and written by Dr. Mallard is a gem. Dr. Mallard has the essence of it. He has gone beyond the literal and given access to what is useful. These thoughts from a Chinese thinker 2500 years ago are as valid as they have ever been and now readily accessible in this new book.

Lawrie Milne, Tai Chi Instructor.
Deep Bay, British Columbia, Canada.

As you read "*Something To Ponder*," by Colin Mallard be prepared to take a journey—a journey that will lead you to new paths of understanding, and unearth the Pearl of Great Price hidden within.

Christine Welch,
Courtenay, British Columbia, Canada.

At a time when my life was very hectic I received a copy of "*Something to Ponder*." It brought me feelings of peace and calmness and enabled me to face new challenges on my journey through life. One of my favorite passages is, "used but never emptied." I believe that the "well of infinite possibilities" can see us through any situation. This is a book to be kept close at hand and read over and over again.

Roberta Nelson
Black Creek, British Columbia, Canada

"*Something To Ponder,*" flows through the mind like water, immersing one in the ocean of the Tao. Unlike many translations of Lao Tzu's "*Tao Te Ching*" this modern perspective removes many of the awkward barriers to it, thereby allowing the poetic concepts to, "explain the unexplainable." Then, one is able to "grasp that which cannot be grasped."

AVANH – artist, Comox Valley, British Columbia, Canada.

Have we lost our senses? I watched a mother accept the flag of her country in exchange for the death of her son killed by a suicide bomber in Iraq. She said, "I'm proud, my son died a hero." As a veteran of the Second World War I could only shake my head at the insanity of it and wonder how it had come to this. I was reminded of Lao Tzu's statement, "After the slaughter of men, how can anyone rejoice?" In this little book, "*Something To Ponder,*" Lao Tzu's pearls of wisdom provide both peace and outrage. Peace that comes with the dawn of understanding and outrage that we consider the death of young soldiers and suicide bombers as being somehow normal, something to be proud of.

Owen Philip Humphreys
Medicine Hat, Alberta, Canada.

Prior to major surgery I became very anxious, nervous and sometimes quite agitated. Nothing seemed to ease my state of mind. On one of those nights I picked up, "*Something To Ponder*". Within a few minutes of reading I could feel a deep peacefulness flowing through me from my head to my toes. My body became perfectly calm. As I read on the peacefulness seemed to envelope me. After surgery whenever I read I felt as if a healing energy had touched me. Whenever I read this book it is not like reading it, it is as if it is talking to me. It talks as if I am the only one it cares about. Its words flow with warmth, and comfort me. And this happens even though I don't yet understand a lot of what is being said. If you are ever a guest in my home you may read it to your hearts content but it doesn't leave with you. One never knows when it may be time to listen to a friend talk again. This is a book that even after reading, you will never be finished with.

Shirley Sanvido
Courtenay, BC. Canada

Colin Mallard writes: "True words are not necessarily eloquent, eloquent words are not necessarily true." My words may not be eloquent, but they are my truth concerning "*Something To Ponder*." Colin has recreated Lao Tzu's Tao Te Ching in such a clear and gentle way. His words settle one into a quiet, simple and peaceful place. Reading from this book is a wonderful way to begin my daily devotions. Thank you Colin, for your inspiration.

Beverley Worbets RN, BA, CHTP/I
Courtenay, BC. Canada

Intrinsic to resolving conflict within, thus promoting peace without. The understanding present from "*Something To Ponder*," is "to realize the utter simplicity of life."

Dave Dalton
Courtenay, BC. Canada

Something to Ponder

*A contemporary version of
Lao Tzu's "Tao Te Ching"
By
Colin D. Mallard, Ph.D.*

Something To Ponder
A contemporary version of Lao Tzu's "Tao Te Ching"

By

Colin D. Mallard, Ph.D.

Wild Duck Publishing
Advaita Gems
6505 Rennie Road, Courtenay,
British Columbia, Canada.

First Edition September 1, 2002
Second Edition November 15, 2005

colindmallard@yahoo.ca

Cover design and layout by
David Dalton of onedesign, Courtenay,
British Columbia, Canada.
onedesign@telus.net

Photographs by Colin D. Mallard
Author's photograph by Stephanie Mallard

ISBN 1-59109466-6

Thank you Mary
For sharing a warm and
lovely place, Ideal for writing,
tea and conversations in the kitchen,
Cowslips and bluebells in season,
And, the gift of a generous
and loving heart.

Table of Contents

Table of Contents continued

Who was Lao Tzu?

According to legend Lao Tzu lived in China 500 years before Christ. He was a contemporary of the Buddha and the reformer, Confucius. The story goes that Lao Tzu became disenchanted with the rules and regulations promulgated by Confucius and decided to leave China and find a place to live peacefully. He followed a trail that led to a pass in the mountains. There he came to the cabin of "the keeper of the pass," who invited him to stay and rest. Sometime during his stay the keeper of the pass must have recognized Lao Tzu for he asked the sage to write down his understanding of life. Lao Tzu agreed. What resulted is now known as the "Tao Te Ching." It is considered one of the great spiritual classics of all time.

Introduction

Forty years ago I came across the "*Tao Te Ching.*" I felt an immediate affinity for it. What the sage had to say was simple, straightforward and self-evident—which to me is the hallmark of truth. Since then the teachings have been engraved in my heart, particularly over the years I was privileged to sit at the feet of the Advaita Master, Ramesh S. Balsekar. As the rising sun illuminates all it touches, so Ramesh's teaching illuminated Lao Tzu's words.

This is not a new translation from the Chinese as I'm not familiar with the language. It came about as follows. From time to time I found myself reading the words of Lao Tzu, sometimes months would pass between readings. Each time I paid a visit, however, I invariably read aloud. Listening to what Lao Tzu had to say was like being in his presence. The utter simplicty of his teaching touched me deeply and a sense of peacefulness always accompanied each visit.

Lao Tzu is known as the father of Taoism. Although it is peculiar to China, the same basic teaching is found in India and is known as Advaita Vedanta, in Japan it is known as Zen and in the West as the Perennial Philosophy.

Three primary sources were used, a translation by D.C. Lau; Robert G. Henricks, of the Ma-wang-tui texts, and the translation of Gia Fu Feng. I also drew on the free flowing rendition of Stephen Mitchell and the translation of Witter Bynner.

The "*Tao Te Ching,*" was written some twenty five hundred years ago and from a context, with one important exception, of a culture quite different from our own. The exception? In Lao Tzu's time, as in ours, there was an emphasis upon rules and regulations that governed just about every aspect of daily life and thus inhibited one's freedom and the natural spontaneity of things.

With more literal translations the teachings can appear somewhat archaic and obscure to those unfamiliar with the basic concepts of Taoism. The teachings are, however, both timeless and universal, and when removed from the trappings of time and culture they point to a profound understanding of life, the utter simplicity of which enables one to live in effortless harmony.

In formulating this version of Lao Tzu's great spiritual classic I used the aforementioned translations to highlight and corroborate key points the master was making.

What follows are Lao Tzu's gems as I have understood them. May you find them as illuminating as I have.

Colin D. Mallard, Ph.D.
Courtenay, British Columbia, Canada.
November, 2005

The "*Tao Te Ching*," can be loosely translated as, "*The way of life*," "*The way of Tao*," "*The way of wisdom*," or simply, "*The way*."

. . . .

A note on the layout of "*Something To Ponder*." It seems that over the years several writers contributed to the texts that make up Lao Tzu's, "*Tao Te Ching*." Some verses seem unrelated to others under the same grouping. The verses that follow are separated so that each page represents a coherent aspect of the master's teaching. In place of the traditional numbering small headings have been added.

In addition, the masculine tense is used but should be understood to represent both men and women.

Throughout the book certain words appear lighter than others. The purpose is to draw attention to a particular word, to give it a kind of subtle emphasis, in the hope it might cause the reader to approach it from a slightly different perspective than the one generally used.

What is the meaning of the word, "Tao?"

A number of people have asked as to the meaning of the word, "Tao." (the T is pronounced like a D) As Lao Tzu states, "The Tao that is spoken is not the eternal Tao." I would suggest that the reader approach this term slowly without knowing what it means and allow it to reveal itself.

Some have suggested the idea of the Tao refers to God. The idea of God, however, tends to create certain problems, not the least of which is to personalize God by creating an anthropomorphic projection. Another is to set up different definitions couched in theology and culture which have traditionally given rise to conflict, and in extreme cases, even war.

In the tradition of Judaism, the term "Yahweh" is used to denote or point to the idea of God. Hebrew scholars understood, however, that God could not be defined or captured by language. With that in mind they removed the vowels from the term "Yahweh" thereby preventing It from being voiced, and allowing It to remain the great mystery that It is.

A similar idea exists in Buddhism in that the whole concept of God is absent except perhaps in the idea of the "Void."

From the perspective of Advaita Vedanta the idea of "Consciousness" is used. When one thinks about it, Consciousness is not an object of perception, it cannot be pointed to or defined, It is instead, pure subjectivity, essential to life—It is life— for without it no perception of the manifestation is possible.

Lao Tzu, had a disciple by the name of Chiang Tzu. I like his approach to language. What he had to say was this:

Nets are to catch fish
When fish are caught
Nets are forgotten.

Traps are to catch rabbits
When rabbits are caught
Traps are forgotten.

Words are to communicate
That which lies behind them
When that is done
Words are forgotten.

*In profound appreciation for the
mystery that is the guru.*

To the beloved Master
Ramesh S. Balsekar

Welcome!
What follows is...

Something to Ponder

The Tao that is spoken
Is not the eternal Tao.
The named
Is not the eternal name.
The nameless is the source of all names
And the named the source of the ten thousand things.

When free of desire the mystery is revealed.
When subject to desire
Only the manifestation is seen.
Yet mystery and manifestation arise from the same Source
Differing only in name.

Mystery wrapped in mystery
The great Tao dreams
And life takes form.

*W*hen beauty is considered
  Ugliness comes into being.
  When good arises, bad is present as well.

  Being and non-being arise together
  Difficult and easy are a pair
  Long and short define each other
  That which is high rests on that which is low
  Sound arises from silence
  And afterward always follows before.

  These are complimentary opposites
  And one cannot exist without the other
  Such is the nature of life.

  The master, understanding this
  Acts without doing
  And teaches without teaching.

When the gifted are considered great
Ordinary people feel inadequate.

When possessions assume great value
People steal from one another.

The Tao is like a well
Used but never emptied.
It is the eternal void
Filled with infinite possibilities.

The heavens and the earth are unreal
The ten thousand things an illusion.
To the sage, life's but a dream
And all mankind
Characters dreamed by the Tao.

The valley spirit never dies
She is the Primal Mother
The conduit of the eternal
Empty and inexhaustible.

Taken for granted
She remains unnoticed.
Ever present and always used
She is never exhausted.

The Tao is eternal and infinite.

What do you mean
"Eternal and infinite?"

Since it was never born
How can it ever die?

The ultimate good is like water.

Nourishing all things without effort
It flows to the low places
Rejected by many.

That is why it is likened to *the way.*

A bowl filled to the brim soon spills
An over sharpened knife soon dulls.

When money and security are sought
The heart is ill at ease.

When wealth and strength are flaunted
Disaster soon follows.

Care for the approval of others
And you become their prisoner.

When work is done without concern for results
Peace of mind is at hand.

When the mind no longer wanders
It returns to its source.

When the body is treated properly
It remains as supple as a newborn child.

When the inner vision is clear
The radiant whole is seen.

*B*right colors blind the eye
  Loud sounds deafen the ear
  Exquisite flavors trap the taste
  Exciting thoughts capture the mind
  Attachment ensnares the heart.

  When the sage governs his people
  He takes care of their needs
  And not their desires.

  By doing so
  He chooses freedom over bondage.

Accept disgrace willingly
And pain and suffering as the human condition.

What does it mean
To "accept disgrace willingly?"

It means to let go of self-importance
And live without concern for loss or gain.

What does it mean
To "accept pain and suffering
As the human condition?"

Pain comes with a body
And suffering from the illusory self.

When the illusory self vanishes
Who remains to suffer?

When life is accepted as it is
There is no concern for the way things are
For when the world is loved as oneself
Everything is taken care of.

Look for It and It cannot be seen
Listen for It and It cannot be heard
Reach for It and It slips through the fingers.

Above It there is no brightness
Below It no darkness.
Seamless and unnamed
It is the ever-pregnant silence.

Formless Itself
It holds all forms.
'Though concepts point to It
It is beyond all concepts.

Approach It and there is no beginning
Follow It and there is no end.

It can never be known
For what It is
We already are.

This is wisdom!

The ancient masters were subtle
  Mysterious and profound
Their wisdom unfathomable.

How were they described?

By their appearance.

As careful as a man crossing an icy stream
As alert as a warrior behind enemy lines
As courteous as a visiting guest
As fluid as melting ice
As easily shaped as a carver's block of wood
As receptive as a valley
As invisible as clear water.

*C*an you wait patiently
'Till the mud settles
And the water clears by itself?

Can you remain still
And unmoving
'Till the time for action has come?

The master does not seek anything
Not seeking, he expects nothing
He is not swayed by the desire for change
Nor does he resist it.

He is the ever-present Consciousness
Welcoming all things.

*W*hen the mind is empty
The heart is at ease
And the ten thousand things rise and fall.

Without exception all things born
Return to the Source
And when they do the silent stillness remains.

When estranged from the Source
Action is selfish, reckless and wild
Misfortune not far away.

When the Source is recognized
The mind is empty
The heart's door flung wide
And life is welcomed with open arms.

The sage, generous and at ease
Enjoys life's great adventure.
To him it's a magnificent novel
Each day a new page.

When life is over and the body falls away
What really happens?
When a raindrop falls in the ocean
Where does it go?

The Tao remains
Forever present, silent and unmoving.

When the wise govern
People barely know they exist
This is true leadership.

Next is the leadership of one who is loved
Followed by one who is feared
And then by one despised.

When people are not trusted
They do not trust in return.

The wise say very little
They act instead
And when the work is finished
The people are pleased with themselves
For the job, they have done.

When the Tao is forgotten
Goodness and morality appear.

When goodness and morality appear
Cleverness and hypocrisy are born.

When peace is absent in the family
Family values are espoused.

When a country falls into chaos
Patriots are born.

*W*hen holiness is discarded and religion done away with
People are much better off.

When morality and justice are forgotten
People do what is natural.

When the idea of profit disappears
Theft comes to an end.

These, however, are outward appearances
Derived from what is really important.

And what is that?

To relinquish all attachment
To dissolve the illusory self
To recognize one's true nature
And to realize the utter simplicity of life.

_W_hen the melodrama of the mind stops
There's an end to turmoil.

What difference is there between yes and no
Good and bad, success and failure?

Why value what others value?
Why fear what others fear?
How foolish!

People are excited
As though at a picnic or parade
While I am alone
I do not care
I am expressionless like an infant
Before it learns to smile.

People possess all kinds of things
While I possess nothing.
I am alone like a man with no home
Like an idiot with a vacant mind.

Others see things clearly
While I am in the dark.
Others are sharp and clever
While I am a fool.
Others attach meaning to their lives
While I have none.

I drift like a wave on the ocean
Aimless as the restless wind.
I have no desire but the absence of desire
I am sustained and nourished
By the breasts of the Great Mother.

The sage follows the Tao and only the Tao.

But, what is the nature of the Tao?

The Tao is without shape and form
Yet, within It
Is the unborn potential of all shapes and all forms.

This Tao of which we speak
Is hidden to the eyes of ordinary men

Where is It hidden?

It is hidden where it can never be found.
It is the essence of life, the Ultimate Subject
Consciousness Itself!

As the eye cannot see itself directly
But only in reflection
So also does Consciousness appear
Mirrored in the ten thousand things.

Since before the beginning of time
The Tao has always been and always will be.
Through It
All creation comes about.

How do I know this?

It's what I am!

Understand this and the mystery of life is revealed.

Bend like a sapling in a storm and you'll not be broken.
Twist and yield like leaves in high wind and you'll not
be destroyed.

When there is no attachment to expectations
The identified consciousness dies
And the joy of life is born.

When nothing is possessed
The whole world is at hand.

The master, at one with the Tao
Is a silent example to all.

How so?

When the ego is gone
Pride no longer exists.
Because the me has vanished
Those who look see only themselves.

The master has nothing to prove
So his words can be trusted.
With no goal in mind
Neither success nor failure lures him.

When the ancient masters said
"Bend like a sapling in a storm"
It was not an idle statement
For by yielding to the Tao
No one remains to be broken.

He who is one with the Tao
Has no need to speak
Yet when he does
What he says is brief
And then he is silent again.

Even in nature fierce winds rarely last more than a day
And torrential rains more than a week.
If nature cannot make things last
Why does man hope to do what nature cannot?

To be one with the Tao
The ego must first fall away.
Then
When understanding alone remains
Life is spontaneous and free
Loss is accepted
And suffering comes to an end.

He who stands on tiptoe
Cannot maintain his balance.

He who walks fast
Cannot sustain the pace.

He who tries to impress others
Is not enlightened.

He who believes he knows
Is lost.

He who brags
Does not know himself.

According to followers of the Tao
This is a feast for fools
It does not bring peace of mind.

And so
The wise do what they do for the joy of it
Without concern for results
And the opinions of others.

Perfect yet mysteriously formed
It existed before time ever was.

It is the silent void
Eternally present
Solitary and unchanging.

It is the Great Mother of the universe
And, for lack of a better word
We call it the Tao.

The Tao flows in endless cycles
Giving birth to the ten thousand things
And then dissolving them into Itself again.

The great Tao gives birth to the universe
The universe gives birth to the earth
The earth gives birth to man.

These are known as the four essentials
Of manifestation.

Man follows the earth
The earth follows the universe
The universe follows the Tao
And the Tao is a law unto Itself.

The heavy is the root of the light.
Stillness the source of all movement.
Silence the source of all sound.

*W*hen the master travels
He's alert and watchful
And when he arrives at his lodging
He relaxes his vigilance.

No matter where he goes
How beautiful or ugly the view
How tasty or tasteless the food
How friendly or unfriendly the people
The master remains
Fully present and detached from it all.

When life is lived in a frivolous manner
The sense of balance is lost.

And as wind disturbs the mirrored lake
Restlessness obscures the ever-present silence of
I am.

The man of Tao lives in harmony with nature
And leaves nothing to mark his passing.
His foot breaks neither twig
Nor flattens a blade of grass.

A good speaker is relaxed
His words, clear and concise
Are easily understood.

A good artist relies on his intuition.
A good scientist is free of pre-conceptions
His mind open to what is.

The master is available to all
He rejects no one
In all events he finds value
Nothing is wasted
And his life is harmonious and full.

What is a good man but a bad man's teacher?
What is a bad man but a good man's charge?

When the master is not respected
And the disciple not cared for
Understanding cannot occur.

Only with respect and care
Does the sublime awakening take place.

Know the firmness and strength of a man
As well as a woman's tender care!

As a river follows the valley
So life follows the Tao
And he who follows the Tao
Is like an infant
Lost in speechless wonder.

To know the pure
As well as the impure
Brings understanding
And an end to judging others.

When this happens in a man
He is an example to the world
True and unwavering
Immersed in the infinite flow.

To know honor
As well as dishonor
Brings humility.

Humility is like a valley
Silent and welcoming
Unobtrusive and unnoticed.

The world emerges from the void
As a carving from a block of wood.
The sage, like the carver, brings forth
The inherent beauty
And does not add a thing.

*Y*ou wish to improve the world?
I say it cannot be done!

The world is sacred.
Tamper with it and you'll ruin it
Possess it and you'll lose it.

Sometimes one is ahead
Sometimes behind.
Sometimes life is difficult
Sometimes easy.
Sometimes one has strength
Sometimes weakness.
Some rise to great heights
Some sink to great depths.

The sage, however, remains balanced
Suspended between the extremes of life.

He who assists a ruler in the way
Does not use force to achieve his goals.
No matter the justification
Violence always rebounds upon itself
And where armies have passed
The earth is torn and soaked in blood.

A good general achieves results
And leaves it at that.
He does not use victory as a stepping-stone to power
Nor boast of his accomplishments.

What he does he does
Knowing he has no choice.
He cares nothing for the praise or blame of other men.
Having done what he's done
He leaves it behind and gets on with living.
He knows all attempts to stop change
Will fail.
Such actions are not in harmony with the Tao
And that which is not in harmony
Is soon swept away.

The Tao
Cannot be defined.
Formless Itself It is the source of all form
From It, untold galaxies emerge
And into It dissolve.

When leaders
Live in harmony with the Tao
The winds of the universe dance between them
And the earth lies resplendent
Like the dew of early morn
Sparkling in sunlight.

When leaders
Live in harmony with the Tao
People need no instruction on how to live
Life happens as it does
And peace prevails.

When distinctions arise
And concepts come into play
The ignorant are fooled.
Yet concepts, no matter how clever
Are like menus, poor imitations of the meal.

Those established in the Tao
Understand the illusory nature of words
And are free of them.

And, when it's all over
It's as if nothing ever happened.
In an instant
Like the clap of hands
The rivers of time
Have vanished in the ocean of the Tao.

To know others requires understanding.
To know oneself requires intelligence.

To master others requires wisdom.
To master oneself requires strength.

He who has prestige, power and possessions is rich.
He who realizes he has enough
Is wealthy beyond words.

To accept life as it is
Is to die with a full heart.
To die and not to perish
That is enlightenment.

The great Tao flows in all directions
Silently fulfilling Its purpose
And forever untouched by words.

The ten thousand things entrust themselves to It
And It requires nothing in return.
The great Tao is everywhere present
Yet few are aware of It.

Implicit in all things
It is the Invisible Source of all creation.

The sage, like the Tao, strives for nothing
And yet he is of all men the greatest.

How can this be?

In the sage, he who sought greatness has vanished
Dissolved like salt in the sea.

People are drawn to those in harmony with the Tao
For in their presence a great peacefulness prevails.

The sound of fine music and the smell of good cooking
Are invitations to enjoy the feast.

But words that point to the Tao
Are empty
And devoid of meaning.

Why is that?

He who understands them
Has glimpsed his demise.

When the Tao is sought
It is never found.
When listened for
It is never heard.
When used
It is never exhausted.

The Tao does nothing
Yet nothing is left undone.

When the leaders of men are centered in the Tao
The ten thousand things are transformed.

To see the simplicity of life
Is to be in harmony with it.
And
When the mystery of life is understood
Who is there to offend?
Who is there to be offended?

The man of Tao is free of desire
Peace dwells in his heart
And all
Is well with the world.

The master makes no effort to be wise
It never crosses his mind.
The ordinary man, on the other hand
Strives for wisdom and has none.

The master does nothing
And nothing is left undone.
The ordinary man does so many things
He cannot finish what he starts.

When a just man acts
A lot is left undone.
When a moral man acts and no one responds
He rolls up his sleeves to use force.

When the Tao is lost there is goodness
When goodness is lost there is morality
When morality is lost there is ritual
Ritual is the husk of reality and the beginning of
chaos.

The master knows what lies beneath the surface
He seeks the fruit and not the flower.

Free of illusion
And with no will of his own
He dwells in reality.

As of old
When a man awakens to reality
The nature of the universe lies revealed.

Consciousness gives birth to the ten thousand things
And the same Consciousness perceives them.

Without Consciousness
The stars would fall from the heavens
Galaxies would fly apart
The earth would be flung from its orbit
And the valleys, teaming with life, would shrivel and
die.
Even the idea of God would no longer exist.

When leaders understand the illusory nature of life
They awaken to reality
And the land is ordered and secure.

When leaders are asleep
Lost in illusion
The land is in turmoil and life is uncertain.

As a mountain is rooted in the valley
And the noble in the base
So the awakened leader
Is born of turmoil and uncertainty.

When such a man comes along
He does not consider himself better than others
And, 'though he may have great power and great wealth
He is possessed by neither.

With the ego gone
He lives an unpretentious life.

Not as polished as fine jade
He is instead…
As rugged and as simple as a stone.

*R*eturning is the movement of the Tao
Yielding is *the way.*

The ten thousand things are born of being
And being is born of non-being.

A true man hears of the Tao
And becomes Its embodiment.
An ordinary man hears of the Tao
And half believes and half doubts.
A foolish man hears of the Tao
And laughs out loud.
If he didn't laugh
It wouldn't be the Tao!

Thus it is said
The path home seems to lead away
The shortcut seems long
Real strength seems weak
The easy way seems difficult
Real joy seems empty and devoid of meaning
True clarity seems obscure
The greatest beauty goes unnoticed
The greatest love seems indifferent
And the greatest wisdom appears foolish.

Strange isn't it
How the Tao is nowhere to be found
Yet from the beginning to the end of time
It nourishes and sustains the ten thousand things.

The Tao gives birth to One
One gives birth to two
Two gives birth to three
And three to the ten thousand things.

All things contain yin and yang
All things embrace their opposite.
When yin and yang combine in balance
Harmony prevails.

*It is softness that overcomes the hard
And that without substance that enters
Where there is no space.*

The sage knows the importance of taking no action.

*To teach without words
And act without intention
Is understood by very few.*

Fame or peace of mind, which is more important?
Money or happiness, which is more valuable?
Success or failure, which causes the most suffering?

He who is attached will suffer
And he who accumulates wealth will lose it.

When content with life as it is
The whole world is at one's feet.

Real perfection appears flawed
Real fullness appears empty
Real straightness appears crooked
Real skill appears clumsy
Real eloquence appears awkward.

Action helps one to handle the cold
And stillness the heat.

And
The man of Tao
Masters the world
By allowing it to be...
As it is.

When a country is one with the Tao
Factories make tractors and trucks.
When a country goes counter to the Tao
Factories make missiles and bombs.

There is no greater suffering than attachment
No greater foolishness
Than not knowing one has enough
No greater misfortune
Than wanting what others have.

He who knows he has enough
Finds peace
His mind is no longer disturbed.

To understand life it is not necessary
To know a great deal.
No need to look at the world through a microscope
Or the heavens through a telescope.

Much learning gets in the way
And the more one knows the less one understands.

The sage understands without knowing
He found reality when he stopped looking.

The funny thing is, things happen in his presence
And he doesn't do a thing.

In the pursuit of knowledge
More and more is accumulated.
In the pursuit of the Tao
More and more falls away.

When he who does the action dissolves
Action takes place by itself.
When action happens
With no one doing it
Nothing is left undone.

When a master governs a nation
He is neither attached to his actions
Nor the outcome.
For he, who is attached, can only obstruct the way
His actions are not appropriate to the task at hand.

The master has no mind of his own
He simply reflects the minds of others.

The master is good to those who are good to him
As well as to those who are not.
This is true goodness.

The master trusts both those who are worthy of trust
And those who are not
In return
People trust him.

The master's mind is as empty as the void.
Being empty he is in harmony with life

People look to him with eyes wide open
And listen with an open mind.
For, as a father cares for his children
So the master cares for his people.

Life flows
Between birth and death.
And all beings are subject to it.

Human beings fall into three categories.
A third are known as disciples of life
A third as disciples of death.

But what of the other third?

The other third?

They've become so attached to life
They are disciples of death as well.

Why is that?

Attachment to life brings fear of death
And to preserve life some men will kill for it.

But in the sage
The personal self has already died
Only the impersonal awareness remains.
And like a man with no future
He is not attached to anything.

Having already died
He has lost the fear of death.
Without fear of death
He is no longer threatened by wild animals
Or the violent actions of his fellow men

The tiger's claw finds no place to tear
The rhino's horn no place to rip
And a man's weapons no place to pierce.

Why is that?

Because in such a man
The identified consciousness has dissolved.

The Tao gives birth to the ten thousand things
Forms them into matter
And stamps them with uniqueness.

This is why love of the Tao
Is implicit in all things.

The Tao creates all beings
Nourishes them, maintains them, cares for them
Comforts them, protects them
And then returns them to Itself again.

Although the Tao gives birth to the ten thousand things
It does not own them
And, 'though it acts on their behalf
It does not create dependence.
It guides them
And interferes with none of them.
Having raised them
It does not rule them.

What a mystery this is!

*M*anifestation is the child of the Great Mother
Learn about her children and you'll learn about her.

What do you mean
"Learn about her children and you'll learn about her"?

Find out what you are not
And you'll know what you are.

When you know what you are
You and the Great Mother
Are One.

Then, all suffering vanishes
And life is effortless and full.

When the mind is free of judgment
And the body free of desire
The heart is filled with infinite peace.

When the mind is subject to judgment
And the body seduced by desire
Nothing in the world can save you from misery.

To see clearly what is, brings understanding
While yielding brings strength.

To use the personal consciousness
To return to the Impersonal Consciousness
Is the beginning of wisdom.

Before time ever was the great Tao existed
Silent and unmoving.

Then suddenly It moved
For no reason
The potential became actual
And the vast universe was born.

The great way is so simple
People find it hard to accept.

It is easier for them to believe
That life is complex
Difficult and confusing.

He who is established in the Tao
Cannot be uprooted.
He who is embraced by the Tao
Transcends time.

When the Tao is present in daily living
Life is spontaneous, simple and free.

When present in family life
The family flourishes.

When present in a nation
It becomes an example to its neighbors.

When present in the universe
The whole universe sings.

When free of attachment
Peacefulness pervades
Seeping into the family
It spills into the village
From the village it enters the nation
And from a nation it permeates the world.

How do I know this?
Through observation.

He who is in harmony with the Tao
Is like a newborn child.
Neither wasps, nor scorpions, nor snakes, will sting him.
His bones are soft, his muscles weak
And his grip is strong.

He knows nothing of the union of a man and a woman
Yet, so strong is his vital energy his penis stands erect.
So complete is the infant's harmony
He can scream all day
Without becoming hoarse.

When a man knows the harmony and vitality of a child
It is a great gift.
When permanent
It is enlightenment.

But

He who seeks enlightenment
Through discipline and
Spiritual practice
Becomes frustrated and exhausted.

This is not the way of the Tao
And he who pursues this path
Cannot succeed.

Those who know, say little
Those who say, know little.

When the mouth is closed
Life is simply witnessed.

The sharp edges are smoothed away
The tangles unravel by themselves
The harsh glare fades
And the swirling dust
Settles by itself.

This is how the sage experiences
The harmony of life.

The relationships of a sage are impersonal.
He needs nothing
So nothing can be added to him.
Possessing nothing
Nothing can be taken from him.

With a man like this
Honor and disgrace are the same.

Being one with the Tao
Is the highest state in which a man can find himself.

To govern a nation, be straightforward
To wage war, surprise is an important tactic.

To become a master of life, be attached to nothing
And allow everything to be as it is.

Why?

When laws are passed
Regulations and taboos enforced
People are the poorer for it.

When weapons are created
The temptation to use them
Is overwhelming.

The more clever and ingenious men become
The greater mischief they get into.
The more knowledge of laws and regulations they have
The more effective they are
At circumventing them.

This is why the sage says

"I do nothing
And people are transformed by themselves.
I enjoy life as it is
And people become upright and honest.
I do not concern myself with the affairs of others
And people prosper

"Free from desire
I watch in awe
As people discover
The utter simplicity of life."

*W*hen a country is governed with tolerance
People are simple and honest.
When a country is governed with repression
People are cunning and devious.

Who knows what will happen next?

Try and enforce honesty
And people become dishonest.
Try and make people happy
And they become miserable.
Give them wealth
And they'll never have enough.

Disaster arises from good fortune
Good fortune from disaster.

Those who do not understand this
Live in confusion
Like fools who demand the head of a coin
While rejecting the tail.

The sage takes life as it comes
He has no will of his own
He does not impose himself on others.

The sage is straightforward without being rude
Radiant and easy on the eyes.

He who governs a country well
Touches it lightly.

He is not attached to his own ideas
Nor does he mold life to his will.
He knows the secret of surrender
And like a tree in high wind
Yields to its strength.

The sage is not imprisoned
By the thinking of others
Nor by the conventions of society.
Not attached to anything
His energy is not depleted.

With a man like this anything can happen.

At one with the Great Mother
He is well suited to govern a nation
And care for her people.

Rooted in reality
He has awakened from the dream
And...
Is blessed with eternal life.

Governing a country is like frying a fish
When overdone it soon falls apart.

When a leader is centered in the Tao
Evil loses its power.

How does evil lose its power?

By not resisting
Its power is soon spent.

How do I know this?
Through observation.

The sage understands this
And governs accordingly
Harming neither himself nor others.

A great nation is like an ocean
To which all rivers flow.
It is a meeting place
Where people gather from all over the world.

As the female overcomes the male
By placing herself beneath him
Similarly, a weak nation overcomes a strong one.

It is difficult to overcome a nation by force of arms
But one can always overcome by yielding.

When a small nation resists a large one
It is quickly defeated
When it submits it overcomes.

Thus it is said

"Those who would conquer must yield
And those who would use force
Are defeated."

Whether large or small
A great nation understands the importance of yielding
And when both nations yield
They get what they need.

*The Tao is the source of the ten thousand things
It is a good man's treasure
And a bad man's refuge.*

*Honor can be purchased with fine words
And respect with good deeds
But, the Tao, valuable beyond comprehension
Cannot be sold
Cannot be bought
Cannot be possessed.*

When a leader comes to power
Don't offer your wealth and knowledge.
Offer instead the wisdom of the Tao
But…
Give it no name.

Why are people so attracted to the Tao?

When one is in harmony with It
What was sought has been found
And when a mistake is made it is simply accepted.
This is in keeping with the Tao.

Let action happen by itself
Serve without concern for results
Savor that which has no flavor
Consider the insignificant important
And the few as if they were many
Repay bitterness with kindness
And force with softness.

Take care of the difficult while it's still easy
And the large while it's still small.
Even the most difficult things in the world
Were easy to begin with.

The master does not strive to accomplish great things
And so a great deal is accomplished.
When difficulty is encountered
He does not pretend it's not there
He sees things
As they are.

Difficult or easy it makes no difference to him.
He know that by facing facts
Difficulties are overcome.

It is easier to maintain peace
Than bring it about once lost.
It is easier to deal with difficulties before they arise.

What is brittle is easy to break
What is small is easy to lose.

Prevent trouble before it starts
Put things in order before they exist.

The giant cedar grows from a tiny sprout
A skyscraper from a hole in the ground
And a journey of a thousand miles
Begins beneath one's feet.

To act with intention brings failure.
Grasp something and it slips through the fingers.

The sage, has no intention
So he cannot fail
Since he grasps nothing
Nothing is lost.

The sage understands
People fail on the verge of success
So with that in mind
He is as diligent at the end as at the beginning.

Since what he desires is the absence of desire
He is not possessed by belongings
And knowledge and information
Mean nothing to him.

Content with what is
He is immersed in what others pass by.
Since he has found what others seek
He can be immensely helpful
But, he knows...
Offers of help only hinder!

From the beginning of time
Masters had no need to enlighten others.
They showed them instead how little they knew.

When people think they know the answer
How can anyone help?

Clever rulers cheat people
And steal the riches of the land
While those who govern without cleverness
Are a blessing.

To understand how life works
Is wisdom.
Wisdom is deep and far reaching
Pointing all men
To the Oneness from whence they all came.

All rivers flow to the ocean.

Why?

Because the ocean is below them.
And this
Is what makes it so powerful.

To guide others
The sage places himself below them.
As the shepherd follows the sheep
The sage follows the people.
In this way
All are cared for
And no one
Is taken advantage of.

When the sage stands before the people
They are not intimidated
They know they will not be harmed.

How do they know this?

The sage competes with no one
And so...

The whole world delights in his presence.

*T*here's no one greater
Than he who is in harmony with the Tao
That greatness is not the greatness
Of ordinary men, however
And, this is what makes it so great.

If the man of Tao
Possessed the greatness of ordinary men
He'd be like them
Petty, insignificant and small.

By contrast, the man of Tao
Is possessed of three priceless gems.

The first is mercy
The second, frugality
The third, not to place himself above others.

From mercy comes courage
From frugality generosity
From humility leadership.

Today
Men have very little mercy
Try hard to be generous
Tell others how humble they are
And always find a way to be first.

This is the way of ordinary men
It is a way that leads to death.

They have not understood
That mercy brings victory in battle
And strength in defense.

This is the way it is
It's always been this way.
It's how the great Tao
Safeguards the ten thousand things.

A great warrior
Does not make a show of himself
He remains unobtrusive and unnoticed.
His actions are not clouded by anger
And when he defeats an opponent
He is not interested in revenge.

A great warrior
Directs his men with ease.
Placing himself beneath them
He knows what is needed.
Knowing what is needed
He takes care of them.
By not competing with them
He directs them flawlessly.

Such a man understands the secret of life
And like a sailboat before the wind
Acts in accordance with the Tao.

*W*arriors have a saying.
"Wait and see what happens
Don't be in a rush to make the first move
Sometimes it's better to retreat a mile
Than advance a yard."

This is known as
Going forward without advancing
Rolling up one's sleeves without flexing a muscle
Capturing an enemy without an attack
Neutralizing an opponent without resort to the use of
weapons.

However
Underestimate an enemy
And you could well lose your life.

The warrior knows
That when well-matched opponents face each other
Victory goes to he who yields.

These teachings are easy to understand
And easy to live by
Yet few understand
And live accordingly.

Since the teachings are generally not understood
The sage goes largely unnoticed.
Not that he deliberately tries to hide, he does not
But for someone who has not heard of the Tao
The sage does not exist.

From the outside he appears like an ordinary man
His clothing is simple
And his actions unobtrusive.
His heart, however
Is radiant beyond compare
He is possessed of the sacred pearl.

Knowing you don't know is valuable indeed.
Presuming to know
Is a fatal sickness.

When one is sick of sickness
One is no longer sick.

The master knows he doesn't know
And that
Is the only thing worth knowing.

*W*hen the sense of awe is lost
Disaster soon follows.

Intrude in people's lives
Compromise their livelihood
Make life difficult for them
And they'll despise you.

The sage knows himself
And has no need to stand out
He knows he is no different from anyone else.

He lets go of what is not important
And is drawn to what is.

A passionate and fearless man
Will kill or be killed.
A brave and peaceful man
Takes life as it comes.

The first way leads to death
The other to life.

But this is not always so
Life has its own way
And even the sage has no idea as to the outcome.

The Tao is always at ease
And overcomes without striving.
It does not speak
And always answers.
It asks nothing
And all its needs are met.

What happens, happens
And no one knows why
Not even the sage.

The Tao is like a net, which covers the universe
Though its meshes are wide, nothing slips through.

When men are not afraid to die
    They cannot be threatened.

    It is the Tao that is the Master Executioner
    And he who takes it upon himself to bring death
    To another
    Seeks to control the future
    And determine the outcome.

    Like an ignorant man who takes over
    From a Master Carpenter
    He has neither the skill to use the tools
    Nor the understanding of what the Carpenter
    Had in mind.

    But

    The tools are sharp
    And one slip could be lethal.

When taxes are high
People go hungry.
When government interferes
People lose their autonomy.
When rulers demand too much
People are not afraid to die.
Not being afraid to die they cannot be controlled.

Why do people care so little about death?

When life becomes intolerable
Death is welcomed
And
He who has embraced his death
Lives without fear.

A man like this makes a formidable enemy!

At birth a human being is soft and supple.
At death he is as stiff as a board.

When the tree is pliant
The wind cannot harm it.
When the grass yields
It is not destroyed.

But, when death arrives
The tree is rigid and inflexible
The grass brittle and dry.

The disciple of death
Is rigid, inflexible and brittle.
The disciple of life
Is soft, supple and yielding.

When a warrior is rigid in combat
He cannot win.
When a tree does not bend
It soon breaks.

The stiff, rigid and inflexible are expressions of death
While the soft, supple and yielding are expressions of life.

The Tao is like a drawn bow.
As the top lowers the bottom is raised
As the height diminishes
The width broadens.
In this way excess and deficiency
Are adjusted perfectly.

The Tao takes
From those who have more than they need
And gives to those who have little.
This is the way of the Tao.

This is not man's way, however
He goes against the flow.
He takes from those who have
Nothing
And gives to those who have
More than they need.

The master, in harmony with the Tao
Gives because there's no end to his wealth.
He acts for no reason
And takes no pride in what is accomplished.

He knows he is no different
From any one else.

*N*othing in the world
Is as soft and yielding as water.
Yet when it comes to dissolving the hard and inflexible
Nothing can surpass it.

The soft overcomes the hard
The gentle the rigid.
Everyone knows this is true
Yet few put it into practice.

When a sage governs a nation
He does not place himself above others
Their difficulties and humiliation are his own.
This is what makes a great leader.

Words of truth often seem paradoxical.

*W*hen a bitter quarrel comes to an end
And peace is restored
Mistrust and resentment often remain.

What can be done about it?

The master deals with it before the trouble begins.

How does he do that?

He fulfills his obligations
Without any expectation that others fulfill theirs.
In this way
He is not disturbed when someone breaks his word.

The Tao is like this as well
It requires nothing of anyone
Yet bestows Its peace on all men
Whether they realize it or not.

*W*hen a country is governed wisely
  The inhabitants are content and at peace with each other.
  There may be arsenals full of weapons
  But they're kept out of sight.

  Enjoying the labor of their hands
  People don't invent things that put others out of work.

  Loving their homes
  They are content where they are.
  They have little need to travel
  And, 'though cars and planes are available
  They prefer to stay where they are
  And when they do go away
  They are glad to return.

  People enjoy healthy food
  And simple clothing
  They take pleasure in their families
  Spend weekends in the garden
  And delight in the activities of their neighborhood.

  Even when a neighboring country is close by
  Its dogs heard barking and its roosters crowing
  The people are content to live and die
  Without the need to see it.

True words are not necessarily eloquent
Eloquent words are not necessarily true.

A wise man has no need to prove a point
And he who tries
Is not wise.

The master possesses nothing
And yet
The more he gives
The happier he is
The more he does for others
The richer he is.

The Tao nourishes the ten thousand things
And causes no harm.
The master acts on behalf of others
And requires nothing in return.

Bibliography

"Lao Tzu Tao Te Ching," Translated by D.C. Lau.
Penguin Books Ltd. Harmonssworth, Middlesex,
England. 1963

"Te Tao Ching," Lao Tzu. Translated from the Ma-
wang-tui texts, by Robert G. Henricks. Random House,
New York, 1989.

"Tao Te Ching," A new English Version by Stephen
Mitchell. Harper Collins, New York, 1988.

"Lao Tsu Tao Te Ching," Translated by Gia-Fu Feng
and Jane English. Alfred A. Knopf, New York, 1972

"The Chinese Translations," by Witter Bynner.
Published by the Witter Bynner Foundation, New York,
1944.

Colin D. Mallard, Ph.D.

Colin Mallard, had from an early age, a deep interest in spiritual matters. His formal education focused on Philosophy, Theology, Literature and Psychology. For many years he studied wisdom derived from the Toltec tradition, Sufism, Taoism and Advaita Vedanta.

A life long search to know and understand himself took him to India and eventually into the presence of the Advaita Master, Ramesh. S. Balsekar who became his final teacher. Ramesh was able to destroy his pre-conceived notions and in the emptiness that remained the underlying reality was revealed.

Mallard, who has traveled extensively, is the author of several books. He devotes his time to writing and photography. He is married and lives in Canada.

*Books can be ordered from
the Internet at:*

*Booksurge.com
Amazon.com
Amazon.ca
Amazon.co.uk*